**DO NOT REMOVE
CARDS FROM POCKET**

A New True Book

NEPTUNE

By Dennis B. Fradin

CHILDRENS PRESS ®

CHICAGO

A close-up of Neptune from *Voyager II*

The Bettmann Archive—9, 11 (left), 13 (right), 15 (2 photos), 19, 20, 24

NASA—10 (top right, center left)

NASA-Jet Propulsion Lab—Cover, 2, 10 (top left, center middle, center right), 22, 31, 38, 40, 41 (2 photos), 42, 43

North Wind Picture Archives—11 (right)

James Oberg—32 (right)

Photri—5, 6, 7, 10 (bottom left), 13 (left), 17, 26, 29, 30, 32 (left), 33 (2 photos), 35, 36, 37, 45

Cover: *Voyager II* picture of Neptune

Library of Congress Cataloging-in-Publication Data

Fradin, Dennis B.
  Neptune / by Dennis B. Fradin.
    p.   cm. — (A New true book)
  Includes index.
  Summary: Presents facts about the large, gaseous planet, from its discovery to the latest findings from the Voyager II space probe which passed by Neptune in 1986.
  ISBN 0-516-01187-1
  1. Neptune (Planet)—Juvenile literature.
[1. Neptune (Planet)] I. Title.
QB691.F7 1990   89-71174
523.4'81—dc20   CIP
                                        AC

TABLE OF CONTENTS

A STARRY SKY

Stars are giant balls of hot, glowing gas. On a clear night our eyes can spot thousands of stars. There are yellow, orange, red, white, and blue stars.

A star's color shows how hot it is. Red stars are the coolest stars. They have temperatures of about 5500°F. The hottest stars are blue-white. They have temperatures topping 50,000°F.

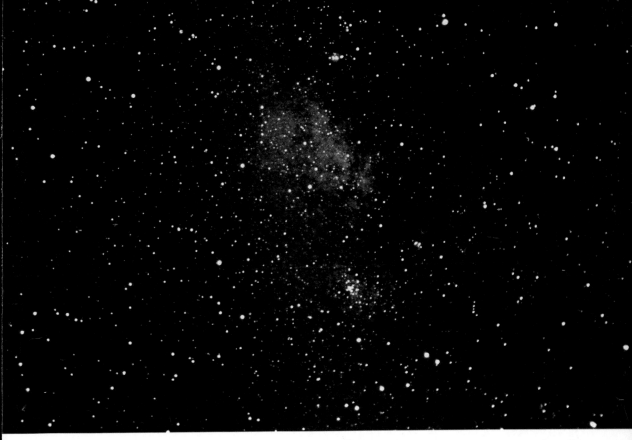

The stars look like twinkling points of light
because they are all so very far away.

The stars seem to
disappear in the daytime.
They are still there, but we
can't see them because
one star—the Sun—lights up
our daytime sky.

5

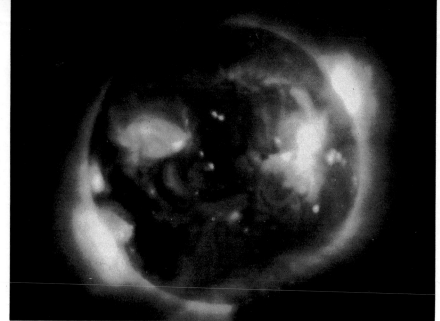

The Sun is
a fiery ball
of gas.

The Sun is a yellow star. It looks so big and bright because it is only ninety-three million miles from our Earth. That is almost next door compared with the other stars. The Sun is close enough to provide our Earth with heat and light.

This drawing of the Solar System shows you the planets that move around the Sun. It is not drawn to scale.

THE SOLAR SYSTEM

At least nine large objects called planets orbit (move around) the Sun. We call them Mercury, Venus, Earth, Mars, Jupiter, Saturn, Uranus, Neptune, and Pluto. The Sun and the nine planets are the main members of the Solar System.

Moons are also part of the Solar System. Moons orbit every planet except Mercury and Venus. Our Earth has one big moon. Saturn has more than twenty moons. The comets and asteroids that sometimes can be seen in the night sky are also part of the Solar System.

ANCIENT PEOPLE KNEW FIVE PLANETS

Four hundred years ago, astronomers did not have telescopes.

Telescopes did not exist until about 400 years ago. But, using only their eyes, ancient people knew of five planets—Mercury, Venus, Mars, Jupiter, and Saturn. All five can easily be seen if you know where to look.

The ancients didn't know

Mars

Earth

Saturn

Mariner X photographs of Mercury (left) and Venus (right)

Jupiter

that our Earth is a planet. They thought that the Earth was a special place at the center of space. They thought that the planets, the Sun, and everything else in space circled the Earth.

COPERNICUS LEARNS THE TRUTH

People didn't learn how the Solar System really works until about 500 years ago. The Polish astronomer Nicolaus Copernicus (1473-1543) discovered the truth.

Nicolaus Copernicus was a Polish astronomer.

Copernicus suggested that the Earth is a planet, and that the Earth and the other planets all orbit the Sun. People slowly accepted this theory as the truth. The Earth orbits the Sun instead of the other way around.

At first people thought that the planets traveled in a circle. The German astronomer Johannes Kepler (1571-1630) showed that the planets orbit the Sun in oval-shaped paths.

Galileo (left) and Johannes Kepler (right)

THE DISCOVERY OF URANUS

Kepler was still alive when the first telescope was built around 1608. Telescopes make distant objects look closer. Galileo (1564-1642) of Italy was the first famous astronomer to use a telescope.

13

Galileo discovered that Jupiter has moons. He found that our Moon has mountains and craters. But he did not find any new planets.

By 1780 people still thought that Mercury, Venus, Earth, Mars, Jupiter, and Saturn were the only planets. Then in 1781 William Herschel (1738-1822) discovered the seventh planet.

Herschel was a German-born musician who lived in England. Astronomy was his hobby. On March 13, 1781,

William Herschel found the planet Uranus with this forty-foot reflecting telescope.

Herschel spotted an unknown greenish object. Over the next several months, Herschel and other astronomers watched the object. They found that it was orbiting the Sun beyond Saturn. Herschel named the planet Uranus, for the Greek and Roman god of the sky.

15

NEPTUNE IS DISCOVERED

Gravity is the force that pulls objects together in space. The Earth's gravity holds us to the ground. The pull of the Sun's gravity keeps the planets from flying off into space.

The Sun's pull on the planets is very strong. The planets' pull on each other is weaker. Knowing the strength of the gravitational pull of the Sun and the planets helps astronomers figure

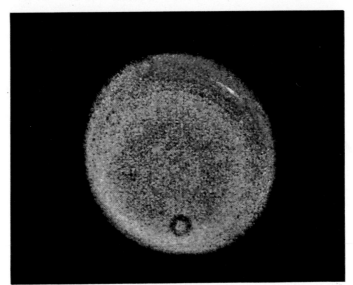

Voyager II
photograph
of Uranus

out where a planet will be in the future.

Soon after its discovery, Uranus was found to be moving strangely. It was always wobbling away from where it should be. Something beyond Uranus was pulling at it. Astronomers thought this "something" was an eighth planet. By the 1840s several astronomers were searching for it.

Not all astronomers use telescopes. Some use mathematics. Some work on theories, or ideas, about objects in space. The English astronomer John Couch Adams (1819-1892) worked on a theory of the eighth planet's location. By 1845 he had his results. If someone had listened to Adams, the eighth planet

James Couch Adams was one of the discoverers of Neptune.

would have been found in 1845. But Adams was young and unknown. No astronomer with a large telescope followed his advice.

Meanwhile, the French astronomer Urbain Leverrier (1811-1877) was working on the same problem. In

Urbain Leverrier

1846, Leverrier wrote a paper stating where the eighth planet could be found. He had picked almost the same spot as Adams! But Leverrier was able to convince other astronomers to look where he said.

On September 23, 1846, the German astronomers Johann Galle and Heinrich Louis d'Arrest used a large telescope to search where Leverrier said the planet would be.

That night they spotted an unknown object that wasn't on their star chart. They weren't yet sure that the object was a planet, though. It was so dim that it looked like a star.

The next night they looked at the object again. It

These six photographs of Neptune were made by *Voyager II* using different-colored filters, so that scientists could study the planet's atmosphere.

had moved slightly among the stars. This meant that the object was in orbit around the Sun. It was a planet!

September 23, 1846— when Galle and d'Arrest first saw it—was the eighth planet's date of discovery. But who discovered it? And what should it be named?

Some people said that John Couch Adams was the discoverer. He was the first to predict its location. Others gave the honor to Urbain Leverrier. His paper had stated where the planet could be found. Scientists argued over this. Today, both Adams and Leverrier are called the discoverers of the eighth planet.

There was a smaller fight over the planet's name. At first, some people called it

Leverrier. But it was finally decided to name the planet after an ancient god (like every other planet but the Earth). The planet was named Neptune, for the Roman god of the sea.

Statue of the Roman god Neptune

TELESCOPES AND NEPTUNE

A few facts about Neptune were learned in the first 143 years after its discovery. Astronomers learned these facts using telescopes and mathematics.

Neptune was found to be very far from the Sun—an average of almost 3 billion miles. Our Earth is only about one-thirtieth that far from the Sun.

In 1930, a ninth planet was discovered and named

Pluto has one moon, named Charon.

Pluto. Usually Pluto is the farthest planet from the Sun. But now and then Pluto goes inside Neptune's orbit. Between 1979 and 1999, Neptune and not Pluto is the most distant planet from the Sun.

A planet's day is the time

it takes to rotate, or spin,
once. Our Earth rotates once
in twenty-four hours, so our
day has twenty-four hours.
Neptune spins once in about
sixteen hours, so its day has
about sixteen hours. Neptune
is so far from the Sun that
its daytime is only about
one-thousandth as bright as
our daytime on Earth.

A planet's year is the time
it takes to orbit the Sun. Our

year has 365¼ days because our Earth takes 365¼ days to orbit the Sun. The farther out a planet is, the slower it moves and the longer is its year. Neptune orbits the Sun in 165 Earth-years, so one year on planet Neptune equals 165 years on Earth. Slightly over a year has passed on Neptune since Abraham Lincoln was born in 1809!

Neptune was found to be very large. Its diameter is

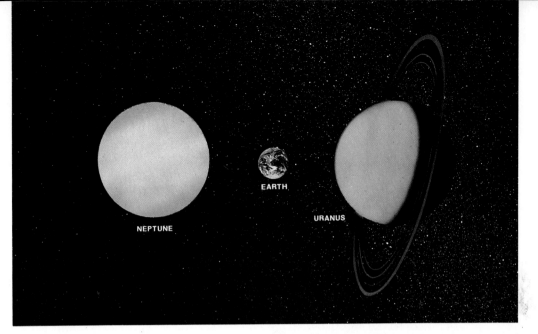

In this painting, the giant planets Uranus and
Neptune are compared in size to Earth.

about 30,770 miles. About
57 Earths could fit inside
Neptune. Jupiter, Saturn,
Uranus, and Neptune are
called the giant planets
because they are by far the
largest of the nine. All four
are very cold because they
are so far from the Sun. All

four have atmospheres that
human beings could not
breathe.

   A few days after
Neptune's discovery in
1846, it was found to have a
big moon. The moon was
named Triton. In 1949,
Neptune was found to have
a smaller moon, which was
named Nereid. In the early
1980s, Neptune was found to

Neptune and its
big moon Triton
(upper right)

Voyager II photographs of the rings of Neptune
taken from a distance of 175,000 miles

have rings, somewhat like
Saturn's rings. Little could be
learned about Neptune's
rings from Earth, though.

Because of Neptune's
great distance, astronomers
knew less about it than about
any other planet except Pluto.
They had many questions.

VOYAGER II VISITS NEPTUNE

The space age began in 1957 when Russia launched *Sputnik I*, the first artificial satellite to orbit the Earth. In 1969, two Americans walked on the Moon—the first

Sputnik I (left) looked like a spiked ball. The painting at right shows *Sputnik* being launched into space.

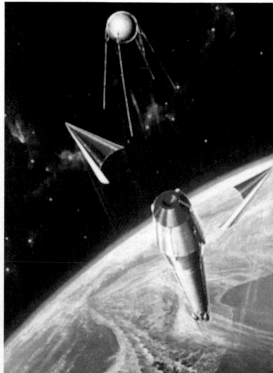

Apollo 11 astronaut Edwin E. Aldrin, Jr., walked on the Moon. The Moon's dry surface is covered with craters.

human beings to reach another heavenly body.

The Moon is very close to us compared with the planets. People may not visit the planets until well past the year 2000. But scientists found a way to explore the planets without anyone going there. In the 1960s, they began sending space probes to the planets. These spacecraft carry cameras and instruments but no people. They send pictures and data back to Earth.

In 1977, the United States launched the *Voyager I* and *Voyager II* probes. Their mission was to explore the four giant planets—Jupiter, Saturn, Uranus, and Neptune. While passing by the planet Jupiter in 1979, the two

Saturn has the most moons of all the planets.

spacecraft found that the
planet has a ring and three
new moons. In 1980-1981,
they learned that Saturn has
hundreds of rings and 1,000-
mile-per-hour winds.

Voyager I was then set on
a path that would take it out

of the Solar System. But first *Voyager II* went by Uranus and Neptune.

Voyager II passed Uranus in early 1986. It found ten new moons of Uranus—for a total of fifteen. It learned that one of its moons, Miranda, had once broken apart and come back together. In 1989, *Voyager II* reached

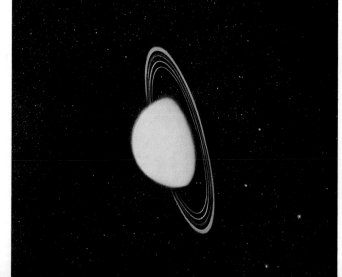

The rings of Uranus were first discovered by telescope in 1977.

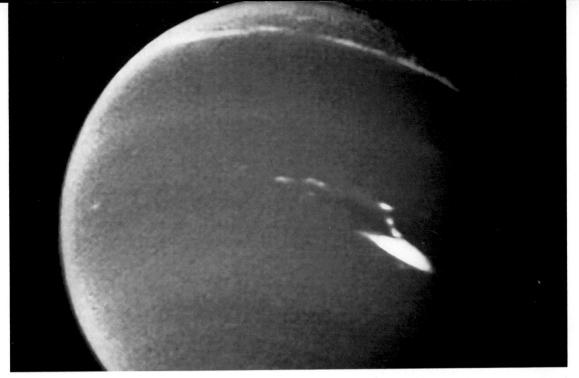

Voyager II's portrait of Neptune.
The white spot is a high-altitude cloud.

Neptune. The probe came
within three thousand miles
of Neptune's clouds.
Voyager II revealed many
of Neptune's secrets.

Up close, Neptune proved
to be a lovely blue color. As

a result, people began calling it the Blue Planet. Neptune was also found to be a violent world. Its winds reach 600 miles per hour. One storm system, the Great Dark Spot, is nearly the size of our Earth.

The Great Dark Spot is at the top center in this *Voyager II* photograph.

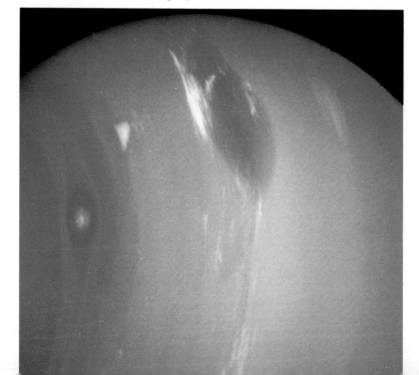

Voyager II sent back data that proved other theories. Due to its coldness and its poisonous gases, Neptune probably has no life. The planet seems to have a rocky center. This rocky center may be covered by a partly frozen layer of water and methane (natural gas).

Outside all this are the planet's poisonous gas clouds—hydrogen, helium, and methane. When we view Neptune, we are seeing its gas clouds rather than a solid surface.

Neptune's rings

Neptune's rings and moons provided surprises. The planet seems to have at least four rings. Some parts of the outer ring are brighter. The rings are thought to be mostly dust. *Voyager II* spotted six new moons, raising Neptune's total to eight.

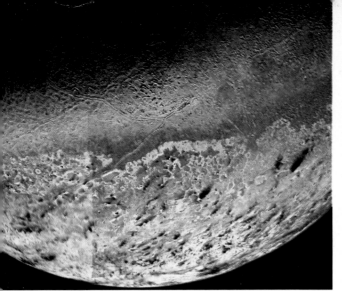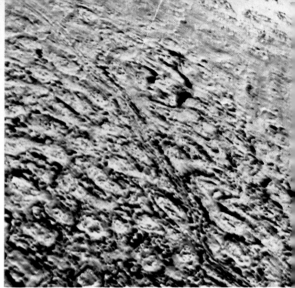

Voyager II photographs of Neptune's moon Triton from a distance of 25,000 miles. Triton has a surface covered with depressions and ridges.

One moon, Triton, has an atmosphere and there were volcanolike eruptions going on when *Voyager* sped past. In many ways Triton is strange. It is the only moon that orbits a planet backwards. All the other moons of Neptune travel in the same direction

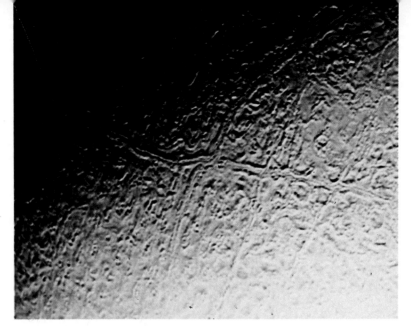

Triton's rugged surface

as the planet. Triton travels
in the opposite direction.

Triton may have been a
planet that was captured by
Neptune's gravity long ago.
It is about 1,700 miles across
with a temperature of -400° F.
Its surface looks like the
skin of a cantaloupe.

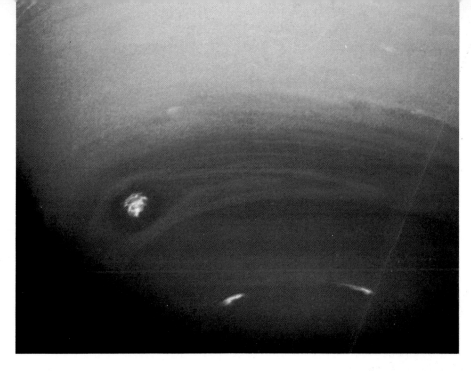

The white spots in this photograph of Neptune are clouds high in the atmosphere.

WHAT CAN NEPTUNE TEACH US?

Astronomers want to learn more about Neptune's interior. They want to find out if Triton was once a planet, and how Neptune's rings were formed. They will study *Voyager II*'s photos and data for many years as they try to answer these questions. And they hope that one day more probes will explore the Blue Planet.

In early 1990, *Voyager II* turned its cameras back on Neptune as it went on to the stars. A final picture of the Blue Planet was *Voyager II*'s farewell present to Earth.

Everyone wonders how our Solar System and the universe began. We can't go back in time to see how it happened. But Neptune and the other

Artist's painting of *Voyager II*, as it looks back on Neptune and Triton, on its way out of the Solar System

planets may provide clues
that will help scientists
solve these oldest of all
mysteries.

FACTS ABOUT NEPTUNE

Average Distance from Sun— About 2,800,000,000 (two billion, 800 million) miles

Closest Approach to Earth— About 2,700,000,000 (two billion, 700 million) miles

*Diameter—*About 30,000 miles

*Length of Day—*About 16 hours

*Length of Year—*About 165 Earth-years

*Temperature—*A very, very cold -360°F.

*Atmosphere—*Hydrogen, helium, methane, ethane

*Number of Moons—*At least 8

Weight of an Object on Neptune That Would Weigh 100 Pounds on Earth— About 123 pounds

*Average Speed as Neptune Orbits the Sun—*About 3½ miles per second

WORDS YOU SHOULD KNOW

ancient(AIN • shent) —very old

astronomers(ast • RAH • nih • mers) —people who study stars, planets, and other heavenly bodies

atmosphere(AT • muss • fear) —the gases surrounding some heavenly bodies

billion(BIHL • yun) —a thousand million (1,000,000,000)

craters(KRAY • terz) —depressions on a heavenly body, often made by the impact of objects from space

gravity(GRAV • ih • tee) —the force that holds things down to a heavenly body

hobby(HA • bee) —something a person does for fun

million(MIHL • yun) —a thousand thousand (1,000,000)

moons(MOONZ) —natural objects that orbit most of the planets; Neptune has at least eight moons

Neptune(NEHP • toon) — the eighth planet from the Sun

orbit(OR • bit) — the path an object takes when it moves around another object

planets(PLAN • its) — large objects that orbit stars; the Sun has nine planets

rotate(ROH • tait) — to spin

Solar System(SOH • ler SISS • tim) — the Sun and its "family" of objects

space probes(SPAISS PROHBZ) — unmanned spacecraft sent to study heavenly bodies

star chart(STAHR CHART) — a map of the stars

star(STAHRZ) — giant balls of hot, glowing gases

Sun(SUHN) — the yellow star that is the closest star to Earth

telescopes(TELL • ih • skopes) — instruments that make distant objects look closer

theories(THEER • eez) — ideas

thousand(THOU • zend) — ten hundred (1,000)

universe(YOO • nih • verse) — all of space and everything in it

Voyager II (VOI • ih • jer TOO) — a space probe that studied Neptune in 1989

INDEX

About the Author

Dennis B. Fradin attended Northwestern University on a partial creative scholarship and was graduated in 1967. His previous books include the Young People's Stories of Our States series for Childrens Press, and Bad Luck Tony for Prentice-Hall. In the True Book series Dennis has written about astronomy, farming, comets, archaeology, movies, space colonies, the space lab, explorers, and pioneers. He is married and the father of three children.